Imagine³

WORKBOOK

Rachel Wilson

Daniel Barber

COURSE CONSULTANTS

Elaine Boyd

Paul Dummett

NATIONAL
GEOGRAPHIC
LEARNING

Australia • Brazil • Canada • Mexico • Singapore • United Kingdom • United States

NATIONAL GEOGRAPHIC LEARNING

National Geographic Learning,
a Cengage Company

Imagine 3 **Workbook**

Authors: Rachel Wilson, Daniel Barber

Course Consultants: Elaine Boyd, Paul Dummett

Publisher: Rachael Gibbon

Executive Editor: Joanna Freer

Project Manager: Samantha Grey

Lead Editor: Yvonne Molfetas

Editorial Assistant: Polly McLachlan

Director of Global Marketing: Ian Martin

Product Marketing Manager: Fernanda De Oliveira

Heads of Strategic Marketing:

  Charlotte Ellis (Europe, Middle East and Africa)

  Justin Kaley (Asia and Greater China)

  Irina Pereyra (Latin America)

Senior Content Project Manager: Beth McNally

Senior Media Researcher: Leila Hishmeh

Senior Art Director: Brenda Carmichael

Operations Support: Rebecca G. Barbush, Hayley Chwazik-Gee

Manufacturing Manager: Eyvett Davis

Composition: Composure

For permission to use material from this text or product,

submit all requests online at **cengage.com/permissions**

Further permissions questions can be emailed to

permissionrequest@cengage.com

ISBN: 978-0-357-91184-6

National Geographic Learning
Cheriton House, North Way,
Andover, Hampshire, SP10 5BE
United Kingdom

Locate your local office at **international.cengage.com/region**

Visit National Geographic Learning online at **ELTNGL.com**
Visit our corporate website at **www.cengage.com**

Printed in the United Kingdom by Ashford Colour Press Ltd.
Print Number: 02   Print Year: 2024

Imagine **3** WORKBOOK

Welcome

A Circle.

1. paint a picture /
play football

2. play a game /
sing a song

3. make a cake /
read a book

4. fly a kite /
write a story

B Write.

make   paint   ~~play~~   write

cake   ~~game~~   picture   story

1. play
a _____game_____

2. _____
a _____

3. _____
a _____

4. _____
a _____

C Listen and number. 🎧 TR: 0.1

☐ fly a kite
☐ play football
☐ make a cake

☐ read a book
☐ play a game
☐ sing a song

D **Listen, read and write.** 🎧 TR: 0.2

_____ make a cake!

Great idea!

_____ fly a kite!

Great idea!

_____ _____ a picture of a house!

No! No! A picture of a mouse!

_____ _____ a book!

Great idea!

_____ _____ a game!

Great idea!

_____ _____ _____ _____ about a dog!

No! No! A story about a frog!

E **Look and write.**

1. make / cake (✓)

   _____ Let's make a cake! _____

   _____ Great idea! _____

3. play / football (✓)

   _____

   _____

2. fly / kite (✗)

   _____

   _____ No! _____

4. sing / song (✗)

   _____

   _____

F **Write the next number.**

1. twenty – twenty-one – twenty-two – ___twenty-three___

2. sixty-four – sixty-six – sixty-eight – _____

3. ninety-nine – ninety-eight – ninety-seven – _____

4. thirty – thirty-five – forty – _____

5. seventy-three – seventy-six – seventy-nine – _____

6. eighty – seventy – sixty – _____

A Find and circle four words. What's the secret word?

s n a k e l t i g e r i m o n k e y o c r o c o d i l e n

The secret word is _____ .

B Look and write.

1. _____

3. _____

2. _____

4. _____

C Listen and colour the animals in Activity B. Write. TR: 1.1

1. The _____ are brown and pink.

2. The _____ are grey.

3. The _____ are _____ and brown.

4. The _____ are _____ and white.

A **Listen and write.** 🎧 TR: 1.2

Oh! There's a tiger. Is the tiger sleeping?
Shh, shh. Yes, it is.

Oh! There's a snake. Is the snake _____?
Shh, shh. Yes, it _____.

Oh! There's a crocodile. _____ the croc sleeping?
Snap, snap! No, _____!

Help! There's a crocodile. Is the croc _____?
Snap, snap! _____! SNAP!

B **Look and write.**

1. you / take photos _____Are you taking photos_____?
   Yes, _____I am_____.

2. giraffe / drink water _____?
   _____.

3. lion / run _____?
   _____.

4. zebras / walk _____?
   _____.

C **Draw yourself in the picture.** Then write.

1. you / watch the monkeys

   _____?

   _____.

2. you / climb the tree

   _____?

   _____.

Lesson 3 Reading

Ⓐ **Circle the word that is the opposite of** *old***.** Underline the word that is something you do at night.

mud   sleep   work   young

Ⓑ **Read and write.** 🎧 TR: 1.3   [elephant   friends   mud   sleep]

Naleku is a baby African _____.
She lives at a home for young elephants
in Kenya, Africa. She hasn't got a
mother. People work at the animal
home to look after her. Every day, they
give Naleku milk and lots of love. They
_____ with her at night too!

In the day, Naleku goes for a walk
with other elephants. They are her
_____. Some of the elephants
are older than Naleku. They are bigger
than Naleku too.

All of the elephants love water. They like to play in the _____. The elephants are very happy. It's fun to watch them!

Ⓒ **Write.**

1. Write two things people give Naleku: _____ , _____

2. Write one thing Naleku hasn't got: _____

3. Some of the elephants are _____ and _____ than Naleku.

4. Write one thing all the elephants love: _____

A **Read and circle.**

1. A snake is **long** / **longer** than a monkey.

2. A mouse is a **small** / **smaller** animal.

3. A duck is **slow** / **slower** than a crocodile.

4. I'm **young** / **younger** than my cousin.

5. My brother is **big** / **bigger** and **old** / **older** than me.

6. My bike is **new** / **newer** and **fast** / **faster**!

B **Listen and write a tick or a cross.** 🎧 TR: 1.4

1. Is a giraffe smaller than a hippo? ☐

2. Can a giraffe run faster than a hippo? ☐

3. Has a giraffe got longer legs than a hippo? ☐

4. Is a hippo slower in the water than a giraffe? ☐

5. Has a hippo got a bigger mouth than a giraffe? ☐

6. Has a hippo got a smaller head than a giraffe? ☐

C **Write about you, your friends and your family.**

> big   fast   long   new   old   slow   small   young

1. My friend and I: I'm _____ than my friend.

2. My _____ and I: I'm _____ .

3. _____ and _____: _____

A **Listen and number.** 🎧 TR: 1.5

tape ☐   cape ☐   plane ☐   cap ☐   plan ☐   tap ☐

B **Listen.** Tick the box when you hear **a_e**. 🎧 TR: 1.6

1. ☐   2. ☐   3. ☐   4. ☐

C **Colour the parts with a_e as in *cake* green.** Then say.

What's the hidden animal? _____

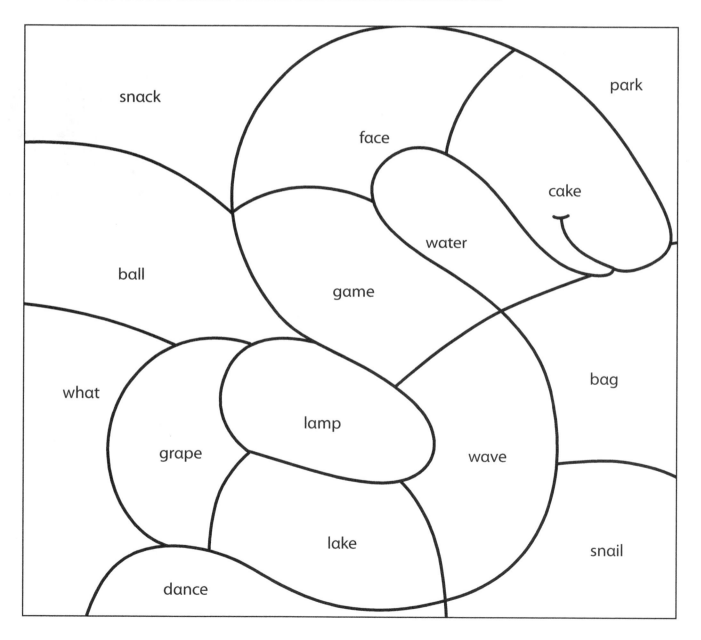

snack

park

face

cake

water

ball

game

what

bag

lamp

grape

wave

lake

snail

dance

VALUE

Be interested in animals.

A Read and tick.

They eat fish and meat. ☐

They eat leaves and fruit. ☐

I want to know what giraffes eat.

B **Who is interested in these animals?** Write the name of a friend, someone in your family or a famous person.

1.

_____

2.

_____

3.

_____

C Draw your favourite animal.

2 Weather

A **Match.**

1. hot
2. sunny
3. raining
4. cloudy
5. cold
6. windy
7. snowing

a.
b.
c.
d.
e.
f.
g.

B **Listen and write.** Then draw. 🎧 TR: 2.1

1. ___wear___ a mask

2. _____ some flippers

3. _____ a snorkel

4. ___put on a coat___

5. _____

6. _____

C **Write the weather words in order.** ☹ = don't like; ☺ = like

☹ _____ ☺

12

A **Listen and write.** 🎧 TR: 2.2

Hey, hey, what's the weather like?

What's the weather _____ today?

It's cloudy. _____ raining.

I'm wearing my T-shirt.

The weather _____ today!

Hey, hey, what's the weather like?

What's _____ like today?

It's windy. _____ .

I'm wearing my coat.

_____ today!

B **What's the weather like?** Look and write.

1. _____It's sunny._____

2. _____

3. _____

4. _____

C **What's the weather like today?**
Draw and write.

_____ today.

I'm wearing _____ .

A **Unscramble the words.** Circle the things you can see outside.

1. k y s _____

2. g o r f e t _____

3. w a i b r o n _____

4. g r h r i b t e _____

B **Read and write.** 🎧 TR: 2.3   brighter   forget   rainbow   sky

What Is a Rainbow?

It's a colourful arc in the _____. A rainbow has usually got red, orange, yellow, green, blue and violet. But rainbows haven't always got six colours. Morning rainbows are red, orange and yellow – you can't see the other colours.

What Weather Makes a Rainbow?

Rain and sun make a rainbow. Bigger raindrops make _____ rainbows. To find a rainbow, stand with the sun behind you. Don't _____ your umbrella! Now, look up.

Can I Make a Rainbow?

Yes, you can. Bring a glass of water and some white paper to a sunny window. Hold the glass above the paper. Sunlight goes through the water and makes a _____ on the paper.

C **Colour and write.** Don't forget the order of the colours.

1. a morning rainbow

It has got these colours:

_____

2. an afternoon rainbow

It has got these colours:

_____

A **Look and circle.**

1.

Wear / Don't wear
your boots inside.

2.

It's raining.
Forget / Don't forget
your umbrella today.

3.

It's cold.
Put on / Don't put on
your gloves.

4.

It's snowing.
Wear / Don't wear
your scarf today.

B **Listen.** Write T (true) or F (false). 🎧TR: 2.4

1. It's raining today.

2. Freddie tells Jacob to wear a T-shirt.

3. Freddie says they can play games on Jacob's tablet.

4. Freddie asks Jacob to bring his swimming trunks.

5. They can ride their bikes to the park.

C **Read and write suggestions.**

1. It's snowing today.
   Put on a coat.

   _____

   Don't _____.

2. It's sunny today.

   _____

   _____

   Don't _____.

A Listen and circle. 🎧 TR: 2.5

1. time / Tim
2. lime / lit
3. bite / bit
4. like / lick
5. kite / kit
6. bike / bin

B Listen. Tick the box when you hear **i_e**. 🎧 TR: 2.6

1. ☐ 2. ☐ 3. ☐ 4. ☐

C Help the bird find the nest. Find the words with **i_e** as in *kite*. Then say.

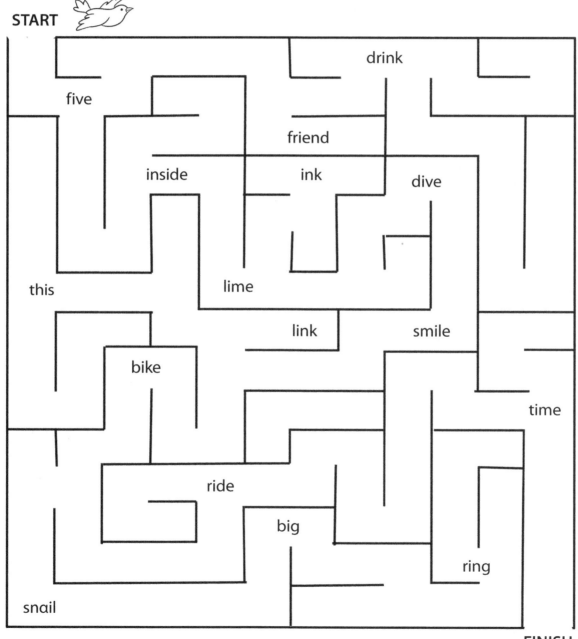

START

drink

five

friend

inside   ink   dive

this   lime

link   smile

bike

time

ride

big

ring

snail

FINISH

VALUE

Look after yourself.

A **Look and tick.**

1. Which boy is looking after himself?

2. Which girl is looking after herself?

B **The weather is hot today.** How do you look after yourself? Tick.

1. Put on gloves. ☐

2. Don't wear a sun hat. ☐

3. Drink lots of water. ☐

4. Bring your water bottle. ☐

5. Put on a coat. ☐

6. Don't forget your sun hat. ☐

7. Forget your water bottle. ☐

8. Wear a T-shirt. ☐

C **Read, circle and draw.**

This is how I can look after myself in **hot / cold / windy** weather:

A **Read and circle.** Then listen and check. 🎧 TR: 2.7

Oliver:	**Help / Excuse** me. **Now / Please** can I see those orange football boots?
Shop assistant:	Sure. Here you are.
Oliver:	Oh, they're too small. Can I have some bigger ones?
Shop assistant:	I'm **sorry / happy.** I haven't got any bigger ones in orange.
Oliver:	That's OK. Oh, I love those basketball shoes. Can I see them?
Shop assistant:	**Sure / Sorry.** Here you are. They look great on you!
Oliver:	Yes, **I'd like / I want** these shoes. How much are they?
Shop assistant:	They're 25 euros.
Oliver:	Here you **are / do**: 25 euros.
Shop assistant:	Thank you! Have a nice day!

B **Write the polite phrases below.**

> ~~Excuse~~   Here you are   I'd like   Please can I   sorry

1. Hey! ⟶ _____Excuse_____ me.

2. Give me that apple! ⟶ _____ have that apple?

3. OK. Take it. ⟶ Sure. _____.

4. I want some juice. ⟶ _____ some juice.

5. No. ⟶ I'm _____.

A **Remember the video.** Tick the things that go in Tian Tian's cake.

bamboo ☐   bananas ☐   beans ☐

carrots ☐   pears ☐   water ☐

B **Look, read and write.**

1. What is the zookeeper making?   a _____

2. How old is Tian Tian today?   _____

3. What shape is Tian Tian's cake?   a _____

4. Where is Tian Tian?   _____

5. What is Tian Tian doing?   He's _____ his cake.

C **Write.**

1. What do you like to eat at a party?

_____

_____

_____

2. How do people in your country celebrate when they are 16?

_____

_____

_____

A **Circle the one that doesn't belong.**

1. rainbow   giraffe   raining

2. sunny   monkey   rhino

3. cloudy   zebra   windy

4. coat   elephant   hippo

5. snowing   cold   hot

6. lion   crocodile   tiger

B **Circle six words.** Find the secret word.

s l e e p s f o r g e t c s k y a f a s t r b r i g h t f s l o w

The secret word is _____ .

C **Look and write.**

Words with a_e	Words with i_e
cake	

D **Look and write.**

1. Is it snowing?

   _____

2. What's the weather like?

   _____

3. Is the snake sleeping?

   _____

4. Is the elephant bigger than
   the monkey?

   _____

E **Look at the picture in Activity D.** An explorer is going to this place.
Make some suggestions.

1. (forget)

   Don't forget your hat.

   _____

2. (forget)

   _____

   _____

3. (bring)

   _____

   _____

4. (wear)

   _____

   _____

3 Let's Go!

Lesson 1 Vocabulary

A Listen and number. 🎧 TR: 3.1

☐ bus ☐ car ☐ helicopter ☐ lorry

☐ motorbike ☐ plane ☐ ship

B Write.

It goes on water.	
It goes on land.	car
It goes in the sky.	

C Write about going to school and coming home.

1. I go to school by _____.

2. I get to school at _____.

3. I come home by _____.

4. I come home at _____.

A **Listen and write.** 🎧 TR: 3.2

_____ do you _____ school?

By bus or car or train?

I go to school by bus.

Then it brings me home again.

_____ does your school bus _____ ?

At six or seven or eight?

It comes at seven o'clock,

but now and then it's late!

_____ your school bus _____

after you get to school?

It goes past the library, the shops,

the playground and the pool.

B **Put the words in the correct order.** Then match.

1. school / do / how / to / you / get / ?

   _____

2. to / do / when / you / get / school / ?

   _____

3. do / have / lunch / you / where / ?

   _____

a. I have lunch at school. ☐

b. I go by bike. ☐

c. I get to school at nine o'clock. ☐

C **Write three questions to ask a friend.**

come home   do homework   get to school   go   have lunch

1. How _____?

2. Where _____?

3. When _____?

A **Find and circle four words from the reading.** Underline the word that has days in it.

p h e a l t h y i m o n t h i r e a d y u s n a c k y

B **Read and write.** 🎧 TR: 3.3   healthy   lorry   months   ready   snack

Bananas are a _____
_____. They grow in hot,
sunny countries. So, how do bananas
get into shops around the world?

1. Bananas start as flowers on a
   banana plant. After about nine
   _____, the farmer takes
   the bunch off the plant. They're
   still green.

2. Workers look at the bananas. If the
   bananas look OK, the workers put
   them into boxes. These boxes of
   bananas go by _____
   to a shipyard.

3. Now the bananas are ready for a long trip. They go by ship to different countries. It can
   take more than fourteen days.

4. Then lorries bring the bananas to towns and cities. There, shop workers put the
   bananas out. Now people can buy the bananas. When they're yellow, they're
   _____ to eat!

C **How do the bananas get from the farm to the shops?** Read and circle.

1. The bananas go by **motorbike** / **lorry** from the farm to the shipyard.

2. The bananas go by **ship** / **boat** to other countries.

3. The bananas go by **lorry** / **train** to the shops.

A Listen and write. 🎧 TR: 3.4

It's Saturday morning. There are _____ on the roads. There are _____ in the streets. The market is busy. The fruit stall has got _____ of fruit. People are buying _____ and hats. People are eating different _____ of food. _____ are playing in the park. It's busy on Saturday.

B Write.

One	Two or more		One	Two or more
1. scarf	_____		4. mouse	_____
2. woman	_____		5. beach	_____
3. foot	_____		6. fish	_____

C Write about your home and family.

1. in my house / person _____ In my house, there are four people. _____

2. in my family / child _____

3. in our fridge / tomato _____

A **Listen and number.** 🎧 TR: 3.5

hop ☐   cone ☐   hot ☐   note ☐   not ☐   hope ☐

B **Listen.** Tick the box when you hear **o_e.** 🎧 TR: 3.6

1. ☐   2. ☐   3. ☐   4. ☐

C **Help the driver.** Make words with **o_e** to fill the tank. Then say.

| b   dr   h   n   r   thr |
| ome   one   ope   ose   ote |

bone

A Who is being safe? Look and tick.

B Match.

1.

2.

3.

a.

b.

c.

C Draw one way you are safe.

4 Growing Up

A Match.

1. clean
2. kind
3. clever
4. quiet
5. silly
6. dirty
7. naughty
8. loud

a.
b.
c.
d.
e.
f.
g.
h.

B Listen and match. Draw lines. TR: 4.1

Anna

Dan

Jill

Tom

Nick

C Draw and write about you and your friend.

This is me.
I'm _____
_____ .

This is my friend.
_____
_____

28

A **Listen and write.** 🎧 TR: 4.2

Growing up, growing up!

I _____ loud at three years old.

_____ naughty at four years old.

I was _____ at five years old.

Growing up, growing up!

_____ quiet at six years old.

_____ at seven years old.

Now I'm eight, _____ as good as gold!

B **Read and circle.**

1. When I was little, I **was / am** silly. Now, I **was / am** quiet.

2. Before, my sister **was / is** naughty all the time. Now, she **was / is** good.

3. After football, my brother **was / is** really dirty. Now, he **wasn't / isn't** dirty. He **was / is** all clean.

4. When I **was / is** little, my mum **was / wasn't** a doctor, but now she **was / is**!

C **Write about you and someone in your family.**

	✓	✗
Me	tiny	
My _____		

When I was little, _____.

When my _____ was little, _____.

A Circle the word that is the opposite of *child.* Underline the word that means *a drawing.*

cartoon   famous   funny   grown-up

B Read and write. 🎧 TR: 4.3

> cartoons   famous   fantastic   funny   grown-up   talent

Charles was a quiet boy. He wasn't good at schoolwork or
sport. Some of his classmates weren't very kind to him.
But Charles was good at art. His pictures were very
_____ . They were _____ !

Look at the photo. Do you know this dog? It's Snoopy.
Charles is Charles Schulz, the creator of Snoopy and the *Peanuts*
_____ . Today, people around the world love this silly,
black-and-white dog, his owner Charlie Brown and their friends,
the *Peanuts* gang.

As a child, Charles Schulz's life wasn't easy. As a _____ , Charles Schulz was a
_____ artist. Art was his _____ . What's your talent?

C Write and draw.

1. What's the name of Charles Schulz's
   famous cartoon?

   _____

2. What's Snoopy like?
   He's _____ .

3. Who's Snoopy's owner?

   _____

4. What was Charles's talent?

   _____

Draw your favourite cartoon character.

A **Read what Sam and his granny talk about.** Join the sentences.

1. What was I like as a baby?

   They were silly.

   But you were loud!

2. What were Dad and Uncle Jim like?

   You were good.

   But we were happy.

3. What were you and Grandad like?

   We weren't rich.

   But they weren't naughty.

B **Listen and write.** Then tick. 🎧 TR: 4.4

Our dad _____ happy with us today. We _____ on a family trip to the zoo. The animals _____ interesting, but my sisters _____ loud and silly. Then we _____ even quiet at lunchtime. Our dad was angry. It _____ a good day!

a.

b.

C **Write.**

What were you and your friends like in class today?

_____

A **Listen and circle.** 🎧 TR: 4.5

1. huge / hug   2. tube / tub   3. cube / cub

4. cute / cut   5. use / us   6. June / Jun

B **Listen.** Tick the box when you hear **u_e**. 🎧 TR: 4.6

1. ☐   2. ☐   3. ☐   4. ☐

C **Colour words with a_e yellow.** Colour words with **i_e** red. Colour words with **o_e** orange. Colour words with **u_e** green. Then say.

VALUE

Be curious.

A **Look and tick.**

Why do leaves fall from trees?

I don't know. Let's go to the library and find out!

I don't know. Let's play!

B **Tick three things you are curious about.**

☐ animals   ☐ films   ☐ sport

☐ art   ☐ food   ☐ weather

☐ computers   ☐ planes

C **Draw something you want to learn about.**

A **Do the word search.** Write.

q	u	i	e	t	o	l	b	a	s
m	z	p	d	l	s	h	i	p	c
h	e	l	i	c	o	p	t	e	r
z	e	b	r	a	g	u	d	a	o
s	h	r	t	l	o	r	r	y	c
p	s	o	y	b	r	h	i	n	o
r	a	i	n	b	o	w	m	h	d
y	n	e	g	w	i	n	d	y	i
s	n	o	w	i	n	g	k	j	l
b	n	a	u	g	h	t	y	d	e

1.

2.

3.

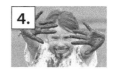

4.

_____dirty_____

5.

6.

7.

8.

9.

10.

11.

12.

A **Listen and write.** 🎧 TR: 4.7

> 1880s   1910s   1950s   Today

1. _____
Cars are big and colourful.

3. _____
Cars are cleaner and quieter.

2. _____
A car with one window is popular.

4. _____
Cars are slow but faster than a horse.

B **Read and write T (true) or F (false).**

1. Karl Benz's car was faster than a bicycle. ☐

2. The Ford Model T was a colourful car. ☐

3. The Ford Model T was good to drive when it was sunny. ☐

4. Cars in the 1950s weren't big. ☐

5. Cars today are smaller and quieter than in the 1950s. ☐

6. Some cars today don't need a driver. ☐

C **Read and score from 1 (I don't agree) to 5 (I agree).**

When I grow up ...

1. I'd like a pink car.   1   2   3   4   5

2. I'd like an electric car.   1   2   3   4   5

3. I'd like a car that can drive by itself.   1   2   3   4   5

4. I'd like a bike, not a car.   1   2   3   4   5

A Unscramble the words.

1. hpsi

   — — — —

2. tiltel

   — — — — — —

3. nacle

   — — — — —

4. tomorkieb

   — — — — — — — — — —

5. nelap

   — — — — —

6. rroyl

   — — — — —

B Read and sort.

~~bus~~ car famous funny kind plane ship silly

Transport words	Words to talk about people
bus	

C Look and write.

Words with o_e	Words with u_e
home	

D Listen and write a word or a number. 🎧 TR: 4.8

1. What number bus stops here?

   number _____5_____

2. When does the bus come?

   _____ o'clock

3. Where does the bus go?

   to _____ Street

4. How was the little boy this morning?

   He was _____ .

5. When does art class start?

   _____ o'clock

6. How does the girl get home?

   by _____

E **Write.** Use *was* or *were* (✓), *wasn't* or *weren't* (✗) and the correct form of the words provided.

1. The school _____bus_____ (bus) _____was_____ (✓) late this afternoon.

2. When I _____ (✓) little, I _____ (✗) quiet.

3. In class today, some _____ (child) _____ (✓) naughty.

4. There _____ (✓) some colourful _____ (scarf) in that shop.

Lesson 1 Vocabulary

A Write the country.

1.  _____Brazil_____

2.  _____

3.  _____

4.  _____

B Listen and write. 🎧 TR: 5.1

1. The capital of _____Poland_____ is Warsaw.

2. The capital of _____ is London.

3. The capital of _____ is Canberra.

4. The capital of _____ is Rome.

5. The capital of _____ is Buenos Aires.

6. The capital of _____ is Tokyo.

C Write about your country.

1. I live in _____ .

2. My country is _____ .

3. The capital city is _____ .

A Look and write.

Keito Maya Harry Siya Lena Sara Lucia

1. Is Keito from Japan?
   _____Yes, he is._____

2. Are Maya and Harry from Spain?
   _____

3. Is Siya from Brazil?
   _____

4. Is Lena from Poland?
   _____

5. Are Sara and Lucia from Italy?
   _____

6. And you? Are you from the US?
   _____

B Write questions.

1. where / Silvia / from? _____Where is Silvia from?_____

2. Megan / from / South Africa? _____

3. Adam and Antoni / from / Poland? _____

4. where / Jack / from? _____

5. where / Mio and Haruka / from? _____

6. Patrick / from / the UK? _____

C Listen and write. Answer the questions in Activity B. ⌒ TR: 5.2

1. Silvia ____is from Spain____ .

2. Megan _____ .

3. Adam and Antoni _____ .

4. Jack _____ .

5. Mio and Haruka _____ .

6. Patrick _____ .

A **Circle the word for an animal.** Underline the words for people.

hippo   son   daughter   parent

B **Read and write.** 🎧 TR: 5.3

hippos   house   parents   snack

Tonie and Shirley Joubert live in South Africa. Their farm is next to a river. They haven't got children; they've got two _____ named Richie and Jessica. The hippos are like their son and daughter. They think that the Jouberts are their _____.

Every day, Jessica and Richie swim in the river. Richie is younger than Jessica. They spend time with other hippos. They also like to spend time with the Jouberts! They come to the _____ every day. Shirley gives them lots of vegetables. Jessica likes to drink bottles of warm tea. She goes into the house too.

Visitors can go to the farm every day. They can give Jessica a _____ and some tea!

C **Write.**

1. What country do the Jouberts live in? _____

2. How many hippos have the Jouberts got? _____

3. What does Shirley give the hippos? _____

4. Which hippo goes into the house? _____

A **Read.** Circle *our* or *their*.

Welcome to Green Park Zoo!

(Our) / **Their** animals are great! It's not like Red Wood Zoo. **Our** / **Their** animals aren't great. **Our** / **Their** fish is very ugly, and they've only got one. We've got lots, and **our** / **their** fish are beautiful! Look at **our** / **their** snake too! It's very big, and you can touch it!

Welcome to Red Wood Zoo!

Our / **Their** zoo is fantastic! It's not like Green Park Zoo. **Our** / **Their** zoo has only got one snake, and it's not scary. **Our** / **Their** snakes are very scary! **Our** / **Their** fish are small, but **our** / **their** fish is very, very big!

B **Write.**

1. **A:** Is that _____my_____ burger?

   B: No, it isn't. That's _____ burger!

2. **A:** What's _____ name?

   B: He's Liu Wei. What's _____ name?

   A: Valentina.

A **Listen.** Write the number in the correct column. 🎧 TR: 5.4

a_e	ai	ay
___	___	_1_
___	___	___
___	___	___
___		

B **Listen and circle.** 🎧 TR: 5.5

1. plan / play

2. say / snake

3. ran / rain

4. today / train

5. paint / plane

6. sky / skate

C **Say and find.**

> baseball   cake   crayon   paint   play   train

```
F  B  A  S  E  B  A  L  L  F
T  B  D  O  P  L  A  Y  F  Q
C  V  I  B  F  M  K  I  Y  X
F  Z  P  T  L  U  B  T  C  B
C  T  A  C  N  W  V  I  A  H
R  R  I  D  Q  Y  R  L  K  R
A  A  N  Z  V  L  H  F  E  O
Y  I  T  S  U  I  W  Z  X  L
O  N  E  S  K  U  J  I  F  N
N  H  C  Q  Z  H  I  C  F  V
```

VALUE

Make friends.

A **Read the story.** How many friends does Tom make?

_____

B **Tick ways you can make friends.**

1. Ask to play with classmates. ☐

2. Help classmates with their problems. ☐

3. Arrive at school on time. ☐

4. Say things like 'Hello', 'Bye' and 'See you tomorrow'. ☐

5. Ask people, 'Where are you from?' ☐

6. Smile at people. ☐

C **Draw a picture.** Show one way you make friends.

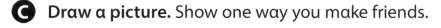

6 Here and There

Lesson 1 Vocabulary

A **Unscramble the words.** Write.

1.  n i n a m o t u

   mountain

2.  g l i v a l e

   _____

3.  d i f l e

   _____

4.  e v i r r

   _____

B **Listen and circle.** 🎧 TR: 6.1

The girl's (house) / school is in the country. To get there, walk down the street and go out of the **town** / **village**. Then you see a **lake** / **river**. When you get to the water, take the **bus** / **path** and go through a **forest** / **field**. After that, you see a **farm** / **mountain**. Next to it, there is a **field** / **waterfall**. Her house is on the other side.

C **List the places in Activity B that you can see from your home or on your way to school.**

_____house_____   _____

_____   _____

_____   _____

_____   _____

A **Read and circle.**

1. (Do) / **Does** you live in this house?

   No, I **do** / **don't**. I live over there, in that house.

2. Does Mika **play** / **plays** the piano?

   Yes, she **does** / **plays**. And the guitar!

3. **Do** / **Does** your brothers like onions?

   Yes / **No**, they don't.

4. Does João **watch** / **watches** football?

   Yes, he **do** / **does**. Every Saturday.

B **Put the words in order to make questions.**

1. do / English / study / you / ?

   Do you study English?

2. at school / basketball / do / play / you and your friends / ?

3. does / in an office / work / your mother / ?

4. do / in a city / live / you / ?

5. drink / do / orange juice / you / ?

C **Listen to Carlota.** Circle her answers to the questions in Activity B. TR: 6.2

1. (Yes, I do.) / No, I don't.

2. Yes, we do. / No, we don't.

3. Yes, she does. / No, she doesn't.

4. Yes, I do. / No, I don't.

5. Yes, I do. / No, I don't.

A **Write.**

> canoe   donkey   on foot   underground

1. I go to school _____ . It's good exercise.

2. You can't drive a car up the mountain, but you can ride a _____ .

3. The _____ is a good way to travel here. There are lots of trains under the city.

4. We go in a _____ across the river to school.

B **Read and write.** TR: 6.3

> canoe   donkey   on foot   underground

How do you get to school every day? Do you go by bus or by _____ ? Do you go on foot? Children get to school in many different ways.

Matheus and his cousins live on a farm in Brazil. Their school is seven kilometres (about four miles) away from the farm. They ride a _____ to school every day.

Alicia and her friends don't ride a donkey. They go in a _____ across a river to get to school. It's lots of fun.

Esmeralda and Patricia go to school _____ . They walk along paths, through forests and even under fences. They walk four hours every day to get to school and back home!

C **Write and draw.**

1. What does Matheus ride to school?

_____

2. How does Alicia get to school?

_____

Draw how you get to school.

A Look and write.

Down ↓

1.
2.
3.

4.
5.

Across →

3.
6.
7.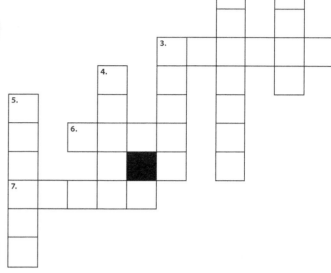

B Look and write.

Go up the tree, _____ the crocodiles, _____ the spider, _____ the window, _____ the bed, _____ the giraffe's neck, _____ the big tree, _____ the wall and _____ the river to the finishing line!

A **Say the words with *ee, ea* and *y*.** Circle the one that doesn't belong. Listen and check. 🎧 TR: 6.4

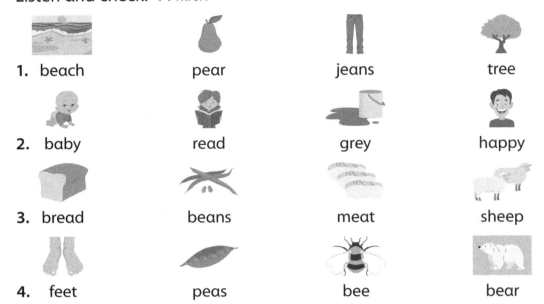

1. beach   pear   jeans   tree

2. baby   read   grey   happy

3. bread   beans   meat   sheep

4. feet   peas   bee   bear

B **Listen and circle.** 🎧 TR: 6.5

1. sheep / share   2. read / red   3. green / great

4. leaf / live   5. please / peas   6. train / tree

C **Help the family get across the river.** Make words with *ee, ea* and *y*. Then say.

j__ns

bab__   dirt__   sl__p   b__ns

VALUE

Help others.

A **Who is helping others?** Look and circle.

B **Tick ways you can help others.**

1. Help someone cross the road. ☐
2. Help your friends with their homework. ☐
3. Copy your friend's homework. ☐
4. Talk to students in your class if they are sad. ☐
5. Say 'No' when a classmate asks to borrow a pencil. ☐

C **Draw a picture.** Show one way you help others.

A **Put the letters in order.** Write.

a. t r s f i

b. c d o e s n

c. f f h i t

d. h n n t i

e. f l t e h w t

f. n n t e v s e h e e t

g. o u t t w n e t y f r h

h. h r i i t h e t t

a. 1st   <u>f i r s t</u>

b. 2nd   —— —— —— —— —— ——

c. 5th   —— —— —— —— ——

d. 9th   —— —— —— —— ——

e. 12th   —— —— —— —— —— ——

f. 17th   —— —— —— —— —— —— —— —— ——

g. 24th   —— —— —— —— —— - —— —— —— —— ——

h. 30th   —— —— —— —— —— —— —— ——

B **Write the dates.** Listen and say. ◖TR: 6.6

1. 4/3   <u>4th March</u>

2. 7/4   _____

3. 3/1   _____

4. 31/7   _____

5. 22/11   _____

6. 10/6   _____

March						
S	**M**	**T**	**W**	**T**	**F**	**S**
	1	2	3	4	5	6
7	8	9	10	11	12	13
14	15	16	17	18	19	20
21	22	23	24	25	26	27
28	29	30	31			

A **Remember the video.** Tick the things that you saw in the video.

forest reindeer milk mountain river boat

B **Write T (true) or F (false).** Then correct the false sentences.

1. Sápmi is the place where the Sami people live. _____

2. Sápmi is in three countries. _____

3. It is very hot in Sápmi. _____

4. The Sami people need the reindeer for transport. _____

5. The reindeer need to walk very far to find food. _____

6. The reindeer can't swim very well. _____

_____

_____

_____

_____

C **Draw yourself in Sápmi.** Show what you do and wear there.

A **Find the countries.** Write.

goutheuknear gentinamsouthafricarjapanothaustraliaelduitalykefabraziliarpoland l

1. ___the UK___   2. _____   3. _____   4. _____

5. _____   6. _____   7. _____   8. _____

B **Look.** Write the letter.

g	farm	☐	field	☐	forest	☐	lake
☐	mountain	☐	river	☐	town	☐	village

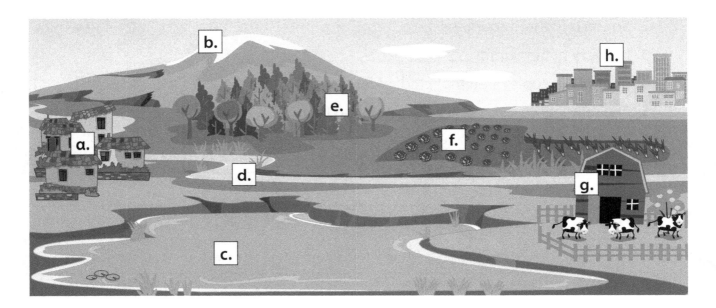

C **Circle.** Then match the questions (1–6) to the answers (a–f).

1. (**Do**) / **Does** you live in a town? a. His name's Lee and her name's Rishi.

2. What **are** / **is** their names? b. No, he rides his bike.

3. **Do** / **Does** Karim walk to school? c. No, we don't.

4. Where **are** / **is** Francesca and Primo from? d. She's from Argentina.

5. **Do** / **Does** this path go around the lake? e. They're from Brazil.

6. **Where are** / **Where's** Elena from? f. Yes, it does.

D **Read and circle.**

This is how you get to my house. When you come out of school,
go **along** / **through** the road and **past** / **under** the playground.
After the playground, go **across** / **down** the park, and then
walk **above** / **around** the lake to the other side of the park. You
are now at the beginning of Spring Road. Walk **around** / **down**
Spring Road until you see some tall trees. Go **across** / **through**
these trees and you'll see my house. It's small and it has got a
blue door.

E **Circle the picture that shows a word with a sound that's different from the others.**
Write that word. Then listen and check. 🎧 TR: 6.7

1. _____ tree _____

2. _____

3. _____

4. _____

7 Helping Out

A **Listen.** Number the people. 🎧 TR: 7.1

B **Write.** There are two items you don't need.

> ~~feeds~~   fixes   practises   takes out   tidies   waters

1. Carlos _____*feeds*_____ his cat in the morning and evening.

2. Haroon only _____ his bedroom at the weekend.

3. Jen _____ the guitar on Saturdays.

4. Lilian _____ the plants in her classroom on Monday mornings.

C **Write two things you do or don't do to help out at home.**

1. I _____.

2. I _____.

54

A **Look and read.** Write T (true) or F (false).

	Monday	Tuesday	Wednesday	Thursday	Friday
Leticia	🚌	🚌	👣	🚌	👣
Isak	🚗	👣	👣	👣	👣

1. Leticia never goes to school by bus. __F__

2. Isak usually goes to school by car. _____

3. Leticia sometimes walks to school. _____

4. Isak and Leticia usually ride their bikes to school. _____

B **Listen. Write.** 🎧 TR: 7.2

✓✓✓✓✓ = always   ✓✓✓✓ = usually   ✓✓ = sometimes   ✗ = never

1. Karim ___usually plays badminton___ . ___✓✓✓✓___

2. Keito _____ . _____

3. Ana _____ . _____

4. Jim _____ . _____

5. Fabio _____ . _____

6. Serena _____ . _____

C **Write about you.** Use *always, usually, sometimes* or *never*.

1. I _____ watch TV on Saturdays.

2. I _____ go to bed before ten o'clock.

3. I _____ do my homework before I watch TV.

A **Read and circle.**

1. Good **leaders** / **recycles** are kind to others.

2. Rubbish is bad for our **leaders** / **planet**.

3. I always **recycle** / **plastic** my milk bottles.

4. **Plastic** / **Planet** bags can hurt animals.

B **Read and write.** 🎧 TR: 7.3

> planet   plastic   problem   recycle

Children can help to make a difference in the world!

Melati and Isabel Wijsen are sisters from Bali, Indonesia. Bali is beautiful, but it's got a _____ . There are _____ bags on beaches, in rivers and in the streets.

The sisters go walking every day. They see plastic rubbish, and it makes them sad.

Melati and Isabel have got a special group called *Bye Bye Plastic Bags*. The group helps leaders understand that plastic is bad for the _____ . Now, people can't use plastic bags for shopping in Bali.

The sisters _____ old clothes to make new bags. They give their bags to shops in Bali. People can use the bags many times. Now, the plastic problem isn't as bad!

C **Write T (true) or F (false).**

1. Melati and Isabel are from South Africa. _____

2. There are no plastic bags in rivers in Bali. _____

3. *Bye Bye Plastic Bags* teaches leaders that plastic is bad. _____

4. Melati and Isabel use old clothes to make new bags. _____

A **Match.**

1. at the weekend   **a.** seven times a week

2. every Monday   **b.** twice a week

3. every morning   **c.** on Saturdays and Sundays

4. on Wednesdays and Fridays   **d.** twice a day

5. in the morning and evening   **e.** once a week

B **Put the words in order.**

1. paint / do / how / often / you / ?

   How often do you paint?

   a / paint / month / I / about twice / .

   I paint about twice a month.

2. the radio / does / listen to / how / often / your mum / ?

   _____

   listens to it / she / every day / .

   _____

3. do / watch a film / how / often / with you / your parents / ?

   _____

   a / watch a film / once / we / week / .

   _____

C **Write how often you do these things.**

1. I wash my hands _____ .

2. I drink water _____ .

3. I eat fruit _____ .

4. I play sport _____ .

A **Say the words with *igh*, *y* and *i_e*.** Circle the one that doesn't belong. Then listen and check. 🎧 TR: 7.4

1. baby night fly ride

2. crocodile smile juice $23 + 58 = 81$ ✓ right

3. my kite angry bike

B **Listen and circle.** 🎧 TR: 7.5

1. small / smile
2. high / hippo
3. five / fly
4. Tim / time
5. me / my
6. write / rice

C **Say and find.**

| bike | crocodile | night | pineapple | ride | smile |

```
U  D  C  N  G  J  Q  P  Q  C
P  R  P  Q  N  I  G  H  T  R
I  D  R  A  B  I  K  E  S  O
N  E  I  L  M  F  O  G  R  C
E  N  D  S  Q  F  A  A  U  O
A  W  E  M  Z  M  I  G  Q  D
P  O  I  I  W  Y  S  U  S  I
P  R  C  L  O  V  M  D  Y  L
L  N  O  E  B  L  Y  X  Y  E
E  V  G  Q  W  G  G  R  A  S
```

A **Which child is being responsible?** Look and tick.

1.

3.

2.

4.

B **Draw a picture.** Show one way you are responsible. Use these words to help you.

at school   in the kitchen   in the living room   in the street
in your bedroom   on the computer

8 Let's Have Fun!

A **Look at the pictures and read.** Write the missing letters.

1. You use this to b <u>a</u> <u>k</u> <u>e</u> .

2. You use these to m __ __ __
   t __ __ __ __ __ .

3. You use these to
   d __ __ __ __
   u __ .

4. You use these to
   r __ __ __ __ __-
   s __ __ __ __ .

B **Listen.** Write the hobby. There is one hobby you don't need. 🎧 TR: 8.1

> bake   collect stickers   do puzzles   play hide-and-seek
> read comics   roller-skate   watch films

1. They want to _____ .

2. They want to _____ .

3. They want to _____ .

4. She wants to _____ .

5. He wants to _____ .

6. They want to _____ .

C **Think of two people you know.** Write their hobbies.

1. Name of friend: _____Aisha_____

   She roller-skates. _____

2. Name of friend: _____

   _____

3. Name of friend: _____

   _____

A Circle and write.

1. He **doesn't like** / (**likes**)
   ___singing___ .

2. She **doesn't like** / **likes**
   _____ puzzles.

3. They **don't like** / **like**
   _____ .

4. She **doesn't like** / **likes**
   _____ photos.

5. He **doesn't like** / **likes**
   _____ .

6. They **don't like** / **like**
   _____ .

B Listen. Write a tick or a cross. 🎧 TR: 8.2

	1.	2.	3.
Ramon	X		
Briony			
Lupita			

C Look at the table in Activity B. Write about Ramon, Briony and Lupita.

1. Lupita _____ baking.

   Ramon and Briony _____ baking.

2. Lupita and Ramon _____ roller-skating.

   Briony _____ roller-skating.

3. Lupita _____ playing computer games.

   Ramon and Briony _____ playing computer games.

A **Write.** There are two words you don't need.

head
interested in
real
sport
stick
teenagers

This is a _____ horse.

_____

Many children and _____ are _____ the sport of hobbyhorsing.

B **Read.** Write a–e. TR: 8.3

A hobby horse is a horse's head on a stick. Hobby horses are ___d___ . But in Finland, older children and teenagers are still playing with hobby horses. They are doing it as a sport – hobbyhorsing. They run, dance and jump, the same as they can do on a horse, _____ !

But do these children also like riding real horses? Yes, _____ . Many of them are interested in horses. They practise so that they can jump very high _____ , just like real horses! They practise walking like a horse. They can even _____ !

a. but they do it with a toy horse

b. and run fast

c. make their own hobby horses

d. ~~toys for young children~~

e. they do

C **Tick the things you like about hobbyhorsing.**

1. The sport is not only for children. ☐

2. You can do hobbyhorsing in competitions with other people. ☐

3. You get lots of exercise with this sport. ☐

4. You can make your own hobby horse. ☐

A **Look and write.**

No, I don't.   No, she doesn't.   Yes, they do.

1. Do you like
playing tennis?

_____

2. Do they like running?

_____

3. Does she like
riding horses?

_____

B **Write the questions and answers.**

1. ____Do they like____
cleaning their
bedroom?

____No, they don't.____

2. _____
drawing at school?

_____

3. _____
flying in a plane?

_____

C **Imagine there is a new student at school.** Write three more questions to ask him or her.

1. Do you like writing in English? _____

2. _____

3. _____

4. _____

A **Listen.** Circle and write. TR: 8.4

1. ow ___snow___

3. oa _____

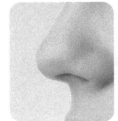  

2. o_e _____

4. ow _____

B **Listen and circle.** TR: 8.5

1. closed / clock   **2.** snow / stone   **3.** show / shout

4. rainbow / yellow   **5.** home / house   **6.** cloud / coat

C **Complete the puzzle.** Make words with *ow, oa* and *o_e*. Then say.

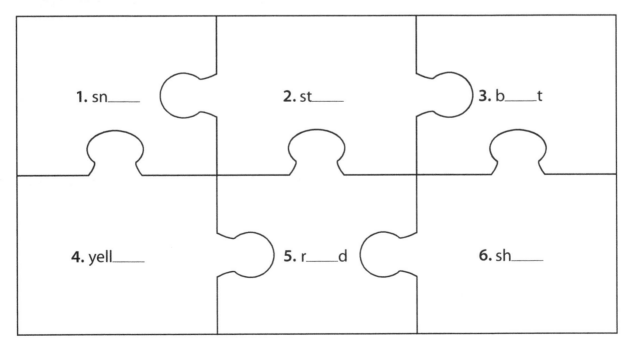

1. sn___   **2.** st___   **3.** b___t

4. yell___   **5.** r___d   **6.** sh___

VALUE
Look after your friends.

A **Which children are looking after their friends?** Look and circle.

B Who isn't looking after a friend?

C **How do you look after your friends?** Write two sentences.

1. _____

2. _____

A **Look.** Find the words and circle.

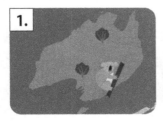 1.
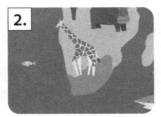 2.
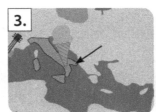 3.
 4.

 5.

 6.

 7.

 8.

l	o	p	a	h	d	m	k	c	w	t	e	c	u	i
a	f	w	u	g	a	z	s	t	i	c	k	x	n	x
k	s	c	s	e	u	g	r	t	a	v	s	d	d	w
e	o	t	t	v	g	n	i	b	w	w	y	o	e	o
x	u	d	r	t	h	q	v	x	s	a	a	n	r	d
m	t	o	a	w	t	b	e	n	s	n	w	g	g	b
q	h	p	l	w	e	y	r	c	y	n	o	o	r	a
z	a	u	i	p	r	t	c	r	j	c	y	s	o	b
x	f	z	a	i	t	h	o	k	y	w	a	h	u	r
p	r	z	b	a	k	e	a	k	s	o	n	o	n	a
o	i	l	g	w	c	i	t	a	l	y	h	p	d	z
l	c	e	q	v	i	l	l	a	g	e	e	p	y	i
a	a	s	e	t	y	o	u	n	g	e	r	i	e	l
n	y	w	r	e	c	y	c	l	i	n	g	n	l	q
d	m	m	a	k	e	t	h	i	n	g	s	g	f	t

 9.
 10.
 11.
 12.

B **Find six more words.** Write.

_____   _____   _____

_____   _____   _____

A Write.

> Fridays   happy   people   shy   talents   talking

1. I visit my grandparents on _____ .

2. It feels good to make other people _____ .

3. The teacher asked the class to stop _____ .

4. My sister is usually _____ , but she loves to sing.

5. How can we help _____ in our town?

6. You can share your special _____ with others.

B Listen. Read and write T (true) or F (false). 🎧 TR: 8.6

1. Christopher Nguyen is from the US. _____

2. Christopher has got a talent for playing the piano. _____

3. The Waters Edge Lodge is a school. _____

4. Christopher visits the Waters Edge Lodge at the weekend. _____

5. Christopher can play one song. _____

6. Christopher likes to talk at school. _____

C Tick the things you like doing in your free time.

☐ playing games

☐ doing puzzles

☐ cooking

☐ reading comics

☐ watching films

☐ helping others

☐ dressing up

☐ going shopping

Units 7–8 Review

A **Look and write.** Find and write the extra word.

1. g o   s h o p p i n g

Extra word: I like collecting _____ .

B **Write.**

> cook   do   practise   water

1. I _____ the plants.

2. I _____ the piano.

3. I _____ puzzles.

4. I _____ lunch.

C **Look at Erik's calendar.** Read and write.

Thursday		Friday		Saturday	
3 tidy bedroom film	play tennis read	**4** play tennis English	read	**5** swimming with Ben and Jake ride bike	read
10 play tennis	read	**11** play tennis film	English read	**12** swimming with Ben and Aron ride bike	read
17 tidy bedroom film	play tennis read	**18** play tennis park	English read	**19** ride bike swimming with Ben and Jake	read play tennis

1. Erik _____ tidies his bedroom on Thursdays.

2. He _____ goes to the park on Fridays.

3. He reads _____ day.

4. He has _____ got English class on Fridays.

D **Write questions and answers.**

1. Karina / like / tidy / bedroom? (✗)

   Does Karina like tidying her bedroom?   No, she doesn't.

2. Peter / like / take out / the rubbish? (✓)

   _____   _____

3. Jara and Liv / like / water / the plants? (✗)

   _____   _____

4. you / like / go / shopping?

   _____   _____

E **Circle the two words that have got the same vowel sound.** Listen and check. 🎧 TR: 8.7

1. birthday (fly) monkey (right)

2. coat   cow   stop   yellow

3. goodbye   hello   juice   time

4. flower   home   skateboard   window

5. grey   night   smile   thing

6. boat   mother   phone   shoe

Word List

Welcome	Unit 1	Unit 2	Unit 3	Unit 4
twenty	cake	bike	bus	cartoon
twenty-one	crocodile	brighter	car	clean
twenty-two	elephant	bring an umbrella	come home	clever
twenty-three	game	cloudy	cone	cube
twenty-four	giraffe	cold	get to school	cute
twenty-five	hippo	forget	healthy	dirty
twenty-six	lion	hot	helicopter	famous
twenty-seven	monkey	kite	home	funny
twenty-eight	mud	put on a scarf	lorry	grown-up
twenty-nine	sleep	rainbow	month	kind
thirty	snake	raining	motorbike	little
forty	tiger	sky	nose	loud
fifty	work	snowing	plane	naughty
sixty	young	sunny	ready	quiet
seventy	zebra	time	ride a bike	scary
eighty		wear a coat	ship	silly
ninety		windy	snack	tube
one hundred				
fly a kite				
make a cake				
paint a picture				
play a game				
play football				
read a book				
sing a song				
write a story				

Unit 5

Argentina

Australia

Brazil

daughter

hippo

Italy

Japan

parent

plane

play

Poland

son

South Africa

Spain

the UK

the US

train

Unit 6

baby

beach

canoe

donkey

farm

field

forest

lake

mountain

on foot

path

river

town

tree

underground

village

waterfall

Unit 7

cook

do the washing up

feed the dog

fix my bike

go shopping

kite

leader

make my bed

night

planet

plastic

practise the piano

recycle

sky

take out the rubbish

tidy my bedroom

water the plants

Unit 8

bake

be interested in

coat

collect stickers

do puzzles

dress up

make things

play computer games

play hide-and-seek

read comics

real

roller-skate

snow

stick

stone

teenager

watch films